COP KISSER

COP KISSER

Steven Zultanski

BookThug | Toronto | MMX

LIBRARY AND ARCHIVES CANADA CATALOGUING IN PUBLICATION

Zultanski, Steven
    Cop kisser / Steven Zultanski.

Poems.
ISBN 978-1-897388-70-9

    I. Title.

PS3626.U58C66 2010   811'.6   C2010-905584-5

Printed in Canada

This book is for
Marie Buck
Brad Flis
and Lawrence Giffin.

CONTENTS

I.

GENERIC HUMAN STUFF

THIS AND THAT LENIN

This Lenin likes Marx
yet that Lenin dislikes the tsar
yet this Lenin likes Woodrow Wilson
yet that Lenin dislikes Stalin's excessive rudeness
yet this Lenin likes the Theremin so much that he takes lessons
    and orders 600 to be sent around the world
yet that Lenin dislikes hunting foxes because he finds them too
    beautiful to kill
yet this Lenin likes German beer
yet that Lenin dislikes imperialism
yet this Lenin likes the concrete details of life, the little facts and
    casual observations which conduct him, without beating around
    the bush, to the heart of things.

We have come to the doors of Utopia.

The lake is frozen over, and the useful idiots of the West skate
around and around it, like officers stirred to grace by thumbnails of
skinny kids in far-off agricultural economies. Ask any homeowner
to step up and will his yard to state power.
                        One of them tastes the snow.
Lenin likes the cold, yet doesn't like the idea of freezing
to death. The animalistic tendency, the sheer institutionalized
modes of report – this is what there is to say. Parts of bits
of Lenin the spontaneous individual move
in and out of focus, resisting the bodying forth of a better daily life
already on the fritz. Sentimentality simplifies the expansive

anti-imperialist project. Sex writes the brim. Either way,
something like hot fudge coats the reader's attention,
pushing like a weed through the top stone of a psychotic
    pyramid.
I am almost free,
so how would a better daily life seem? Would it be more or less
latently erotic than grocery shopping? Would I flirt with the
    salesperson
in the same shy, objective way? His monocle
                                            generates heat.
        The hearts of engineers keep on bursting. Now then,
violent past, unhand me! Grace is the power
and authority to execute justice. Simultaneously my father loves
me and his likeness. So hold out your hand,
generate heat,
hold it out to materialism. We will
begin with being, abstract being:
to make practice into a criterion of truth.

This Lenin likes popular support
yet that Lenin dislikes the liquidators
yet this Lenin likes vodka with his caviar
yet that Lenin dislikes capitalism
yet this Lenin likes to make lists of enemies
yet that Lenin dislikes the economists' struggle for reforms
    which degrade social democratic politics
yet this Lenin likes to gaze into the distance
yet that Lenin dislikes Futurism
yet this Lenin likes white wine with his caviar.

The lake, stagnant in its worsening, dust what blows
across the algae as a plume of white smoke billowing

                    formats the night.
As in the beloved old hymns
it puffs upward, the way a bubble floats in water, as if shoved
from behind, probably by someone who is also being shoved
        from behind,
in a chain of ascensions, as you go.
                    You go on a fishing trip.
The worker-philosopher goes with you, rowing,
making nothing to move from its politicized way.
But row for you? Nuh-uh.
For you to take the opportunities of white people
and understand them to death, this is not why I do
what I do, stowing away at least $40 in benefits
in three child-sized urns. Professor of professor,
you have brought 4,000 years of written history
to just this moment,
to the pinnacle of your detainee's skin-flute. And here
you go – into the era,
my male contractor, my love,
            ready to concern yourself with all
            of the concepts and themes elaborated below,
            ready to become generically unique
to your generation. They shun you, truth warrior.
For when you acted wrongly, it was merely
                    a metaphor.
When you bombed the Times Square recruiting station, I
        thought
it was an anti-war statement, but no –
you were only trying to reduce presence
to its smallest possible quantity. From on high, a tiny black dot
        in the sky,
flying from the point of view of time immemorial,

we see everything from the point of view of political expediency,
as if to say: Let's get into a fight, and see what happens.

"The Engine of Communism," by Dean Koontz.

The stakes of
pluralist juice-box art.

These things speak of a voice. Then
this speaking coalesces into an elementary drama between
equals, i.e. opposites, as a way of making sense of the peaks
and valleys of this, the most trivial of workweeks, the week
in which I retype my check but don't sign the name. Where
the kind of labor that makes co-workers into co-conspirators is,
	right there –
that is where the lake swallows you up, just
at the mouth of a profoundly subjective analysis of Stalinist
	ecology,
just at the edge of a boring sexual encounter that rings
	absolutely true.

> The air is cold,
> the wind is fierce.
> Yet you stand
> there with your beast.
> You know that life
> will soon end
> yet you show
> only the sign of death.
> Your beast talks for you whilst you hide behind him.
> Unknowing and unresponsive,
> your death is meaningless,

yet your life is eventful.
How do you stand?
You sit there without feeling.
Motionless you sit by your fiery beast,
snuggled up tight.
For you to die would be so great.

I like you, you are the only democratic presidential candidate
    with enough guts
to come in here, beautiful and neat. I am happiest with you
    around, lost
to silence or solitude. But whose silence or solitude
is
this? Some capitalist's?

Can you root out the banks of our
youth?
A rich kid
melts into something simpler,
like a cavity,

shut
or emptied out.

You, however, my wife and hero,
lick the bottom of the bowl
        of low-carb chocolate buttercream frosting,
        the way you lick the bottom of my footsie-wootsies.
You must be boy-crazy, Washington, to go all the way down.

Perturbed, juiced up, single.
I, rotten liberalism, with my negative values of freedom,

am juiced up. The single most annoying political catchphrase
of all time runs through your head like ticker tape, or
the refrain of a popular song. What is it again?
Rule of law, unhand me! I mean
handle me, for I am stupid in the sense that
whoever is unable to understand general principles
is bound to make mistakes and, in specific, wander in the dark.
Lenin likes this too. Yet
I recently learned that Lenin likes ice cream. I like ice cream too.

This Lenin likes to ride bicycles
yet that Lenin dislikes eclecticism
yet this Lenin likes sweet tea
yet that Lenin dislikes elements of mimicry
yet this Lenin likes children
yet that Lenin dislikes the bourgeoisie
yet this Lenin likes to help acquaintances in trouble
yet that Lenin dislikes the rich who buy up grain during a
    famine only to sell it at steep prices
yet this Lenin likes mushroom hunting
yet that Lenin dislikes children
yet this Lenin likes Coke
yet that Lenin dislikes democracy
yet this Lenin likes industrialization.

This Lenin dislikes the theorizing intelligentsia
yet that Lenin likes spontaneous mass strikes
yet this Lenin dislikes communism in one country
yet that Lenin likes global revolution
yet this Lenin dislikes World War I
yet that Lenin likes the outbreak of World War I and hopes that
    it will be long and devastating

yet this Lenin dislikes pacifism
yet that Lenin likes to use money
yet this Lenin dislikes personality cults
yet that Lenin likes peace.

    I do what I want
    to do on the lake.
    I row my opportunist's boat ashore.

Worsening,
        my elegy
gets worse. The home state
organs

of class rule, a private space
of oppression
of one class by another.

    It is administered order
    which legalizes this
    oppression

    by moderating the conflict
    between classes.
            In my
    opinion, Coke is better.

    Civilized society splits
    into irreconcilable classes
    until a star arises

    like a special power.

Every revolution
shows us

the naked class struggle,
the self
freed from self

features
leaking. Withering away
stills

the star.
Revolution alone abolishes
    the state
as state. The general star,

i.e. the most complete democracy,
can only wither away. The home state
eats through you

like
a violence – i.e,
all sides of the process.

Lenin used to be very small. But he is very strong now.

This Lenin likes a militant party
yet that Lenin dislikes opportunism
yet this Lenin likes dialectics
yet that Lenin dislikes spontaneity
yet this Lenin likes documentary films projected to piano
    accompaniment

yet that Lenin dislikes gold
yet this Lenin likes evening walks
yet that Lenin dislikes me and my brother for smoking weed
yet this Lenin likes to build socialism on the foundation of free
    men and political democracy
yet that Lenin dislikes nationalism
yet this Lenin likes professional revolutionaries
yet that Lenin dislikes what he sees.

Yo. The lake runs the gamut, from motorboats to jet skis,
from crystal clear rivers to spectacular waterfalls to where,
on the highest foot of the highest hill, the continuous tomb sits
in a belt of forest. Water sits there too,
a rich, milky blue that might be described as atomic, opening
around picturesque villages like a diorama. Speed boating
is one of the most popular activities and you do it happily,
hopping over bits of waves in a white rented thingy,
radio blasting "The Internationale." Did you know?
Lenin likes trials
more than he likes executions,
                    yet Lenin
dislikes emotionalism. And with the winter,
things freeze up. The lake ices the river it gathers at the nape,
carrying it like the Madonna figure to an alternate church.
A found gate opens, artery of commerce, swings into the
    elimination
of the police and army. You walk through to the tomb,
unclear about exactly what it is you peep: the uncool truth
of an orange-tinted face bathed in a halo of light, the uncool truth
of breaking the glass to get the face off.
The best way to characterize it would probably
be to oppose a form of unbridled sexual freedom to a form

of colonial rule characterized by unbridled sexual freedom.
But who will fuck whom in this new philosophical order?
Who will plumb the depths of whom else?
Without a sign, Lenin up and plumbed contemporary art
not only for ideas but for commodities that might, by a burst
of prodigious negation, resolve reason into merely a redundant act,
the chronic bed-wetting of my aesthetic by the purges. The end.

Some years there was enough water to permit skating,
but most times when the revolution came, out of the blue,
I felt left out and hurt. The beast does not have much to do
    with me.
Really he desires only to pleasure, to excite a rigorous domestic
    aplomb
that can swallow up any lingering lower priorities
and restore a barely sufficient desire to live. Ask a homeowner
for a touch of the evidence
                  once. Ask me about
what I can do with you. I can jump up and holler "whoo-hoo!"
I can dart fifty paces forward. I can be
slightly annoying, like effortless love or a funny-sounding squeak.
I can shut.
I can write all this out or scrap the whole project. These are my
    non-options.
Yet representing night and day changes nothing – does not smooth
the officers' blade-squiggles from ice, does not retrieve from
    memory
the literary equivalent of a pattern found in nature
but somehow not found in you. I rejected the arbitrary, and
    now look:
a dump.
We have come yet again to the doors of Utopia. The end.

1. When was Lenin born?

A. On April 23,1870
B. On April 22, 1870
C. On April 22, 1860

2. What was Lenin always ready to do?

A. Help his classmates with their foreign languages.
B. Help his classmates with their work.
C. Help his classmates with their studies.

3. Who did Lenin like to talk with?

A. Workers and farmers.
B. Students.
C. Officers.

4. Which is right?

A. Lenin wasn't a kind man.
B. Lenin was a hard worker.
C. Lenin didn't like foreign languages.

5. Lenin didn't leave today's work for tomorrow, did he?

A. Yes, he did.
B. No, he didn't.
C. Yes, he didn't.

ANAL CARS / ART GARFUNKEL

Anal Ram

Anal Compass

Anal Passport

Anal Dart

Anal M151A1C

Anal Eclipse

Anal Beagle

Anal Citation

Anal Quest

Anal Wrangler

Anal Outback

Anal Park Avenue Essence

Anal Grand Cherokee

Anal Liberty

Anal 410 Superamerica

Anal Fox

Anal Armada

Anal Accord

Anal Commander

Anal Patriot

Anal Quantum

Anal Conquest

Anal Airflow

Anal F 500 Mind

Anal Forester

Anal Mystique

Anal Star Chief Executive

Anal Astro

Anal Insight

Anal Fury

Anal Sportsman

Anal Colt

Anal Model-T

Anal Odyssey

Anal Arnage Drophead Coupe

Anal Rabbit

Anal Intrigue

Anal Celebrity

Anal Villager

Anal 600

Anal Imperial

Anal Prius

Anal Crown

Anal Focus

Anal Trailblazer

Anal Echo

Anal Formula Junior

Anal Viper

Anal Ranger

Anal Camry

Anal Civic

Anal Breeze

Anal Bongo Brawny

Anal Sequoia

Anal Contour

Anal Outlook

Anal Town and Country

Anal Excursion

Anal Prelude

Anal Century

Fountain Garfunkel

The Luncheon on the Grass Garfunkel

Rhythm o Garfunkel

Persistence of Memory Garfunkel

Transfiguration Garfunkel

Seedbed Garfunkel

The Kiss Garfunkel

Untilted Garfunkel

A Leap Into the Void Garfunkel

Meat Joy Garfunkel

A Cottage on Fire Garfunkel

The Assumption of the Virgin Garfunkel

Cain, or Hitler in Hell Garfunkel

Bible Quilt Garfunkel

Victory Over the Sun Garfunkel

1957-D No. 1 Garfunkel

TV Bra for Living Sculpture Garfunkel

Europe After the Rain II Garfunkel

Cowboy with Cigarette Garfunkel

Creation of Man Garfunkel

Guernica Garfunkel

Migrant Mother Garfunkel

Stormtroops Advancing Under Gas Garfunkel

Iron Curtain Garfunkel

White on White Garfunkel

Form Derived From a Cube Garfunkel

The Thinker Garfunkel

The Ambassadors Garfunkel

No. 14 (Browns over Dark) Garfunkel

The Human Condition Garfunkel

Merzbau Garfunkel

Flag Garfunkel

Saturn Devouring His Son Garfunkel

Blue Nudes Garfunkel

Rain, Steam and Speed – The Great Western Railway Garfunkel

Woman V Garfunkel

For the Love of God Garfunkel

Fall of the Damned Garfunkel

Acid Box Garfunkel

The Garden of Delights Garfunkel

Lights Going On and Off Garfunkel

Mona Lisa Garfunkel

Head IV Garfunkel

Not There-Here Garfunkel

Shotgun Hospitality Garfunkel

Erased De Kooning Drawing Garfunkel

Cut Piece Garfunkel

Mao Garfunkel

Apollo and the Artist Garfunkel

Cloud Shepard Garfunkel

Day in the Life of a Girl Garfunkel

Birth of Venus Garfunkel

Nude Descending a Staircase Garfunkel

American Gothic Garfunkel

Action Pants: Genital Panic Garfunkel

Maman Garfunkel

Hermes and Dionysus Garfunkel

Darkytown Rebellion Garfunkel

Santa Claus with a Buttplug Garfunkel

Starry Night Garfunkel

Oak Leaves Pink and Grey Garfunkel

Judenplatz Holocaust Memorial Garfunkel

King Kong Garfunkel

Portraits of V.I. Lenin in the Style of Jackson Pollack Garfunkel

Profit 1 Garfunkel

The Scream Garfunkel

MY BEST FRIENDS

Steven "Personal Growth" Zultanski
     buys a Pabst for
Steven "The Thing Humans Do Best" Zultanski
     who buys a Heineken for
Steven "Quality Reproductions" Zultanski
     who buys a Michelob Golden Draft for
Steven "Play Date" Zultasnki
     who buys an Old Milwaukee Ice for
Steven "The Terms of Fanaticism" Zultanski
     who buys a Blue Moon for
Steven "Judge" Zultanski
     who buys a Rogue Dead Guy Ale for
Steven "New Romantic Style" Zultanski
     who buys a Left Hand Porter for
Steven "Filthy Mouth Belies a Gentle Spirit" Zultanski
     who buys a 2-Headed Beast for
Steven "Jazz For the People" Zultanski
     who buys a Miller High Life for
Steven "Degree of Bunching" Zultanski
     who buys a Sam Adams Cherry Wheat for
Steven "I Like Bono" Zultanski
     who buys a Brooklyn Lager for
Steven "Fissures" Zultanski
     who buys a Hoegaarden Belgian White for
Steven "Two Million People" Zultanski
     who buys a Corona Extra for
Steven "Nice Story in BusinessWeek on Doing Great" Zultanski
     who buys a Harpoon UFO for

Steven "Good Eats" Zultanski

who buys an Ayinger Celebrator Dopplebock Aying for

Steven "All Forms of Art" Zultanski

who buys a Stella Artois for

Steven "Slip of the Tongue" Zultanski

who buys a Newcastle Brown Ale for

Steven "Interested in Zen" Zultanski

who buys a Magic Hat Fat Angel for

Steven "The Unofficial Dow Jones Webmaster" Zultanski

who buys a Victory Hop Devil for

Steven "Your Future Roommate" Zultanski

who buys a Ruddles for

Steven "Coach Steve" Zultanski

who buys a Smuttynose Old Brown Dog for

Steven "Conservative Parents" Zultanski

who buys a Red Stripe for

Steven "Nuclear Holocausts of Laughter" Zultanski

who buys a Mike's Hard Lemonade for

Steven "Unique Party Experience" Zultanski

who buys a Sierra Nevada Porter for

Steven "Manic Restlessness Now Proves Heroic" Zultanski

who buys a Paper City Dam Ale for

Steven "Profanity" Zultanski

who buys a Flying Dog in Heat Wheat for

Steven "Dissatisfied and Unappreciated at Work" Zultanski

who buys a Youngs Double Chocolate Stout for

Steven "Simulation-Event" Zultanski

who buys a Rolling Rock for

Steven "Where the Middle Class Went" Zultanski

who buys a Dark Lord Imperial Stout for

Steven "The Better Half" Zultanski

who buys a Budweiser for

Steven "Series of Hilarious One-Liners" Zultanski
     who buys a Beck's for
Steven "Kind of Rough" Zultanski
     who buys a Natural Light for
Steven "Tribal Tattoo" Zultanski
     who buys an Old Engine Oil for
Steven "A Sober Path" Zultanski
     who buys an Arrogant Bastard for
Steven "Dads and Bachelors" Zultanski
     who buys a Moosehead for
Steven "Perfect Crystal" Zultanski
     who buys a Tsing Tao for
Steven "The Whole Package" Zultanski
     who buys a Dirty Dicks Ale for
Steven "200 Chinese Graduate Students" Zultanski
     who buys a Guinness for
Steven "Unprofessional Conduct" Zultanski
     who buys a St. Pauli Girl Dark for
Steven "Mini-Frankenstein" Zultanski
     who buys a Sapporo for
Steven "Total Anonymity" Zultanski
     who buys a Killian's Wild Honey for
Steven "His Entertainment Weekly Drops to His Lap" Zultanski
     who buys a Ipswich Dark Growler for
Steven "Violent Resurrection" Zultanski
     who buys a Saranac Season's Best for
Steven "Tears of Sadness" Zultanski
     who buys a Pyramid Snowcap for
Steven "The Straight Horn" Zultanski
     who buys a Hammer & Nail Brown Ale for
Steven "Your First Born Child" Zultanski
     who buys a Slop Bucket for

Steven "No Relation to Humanization" Zultanski
    who buys an Extra Special Bitter for
Steven "Lyrics That Say Something" Zultanski
    who buys a Modelo Especial for
Steven "Social Constructivism" Zultanski
    who buys a Yuengling for
Steven "The Public Mind" Zultanski
    who buys a Hurricane Ice for
Steven "Kit and Kaboodle" Zultanski
    who buys a Duck's Breath for
Steven "Encased in Resin" Zultasnki
    who buys a Dos Equis XX Special Lager for
Steven "International Law" Zultanski
    who buys a Keystone Light for
Steven "The Problem With Being a Thing" Zultanski
    who buys a Steel Reserve High Gravity Lager for
Steven "Denial of Human Nature" Zultanski
    who buys a Sparks for
Steven "Talent War" Zultanski
    who buys a Shiner Bock for
Steven "Proustian Closure" Zultanski
    who buys a Negra Modelo for
Steven "How the Mind Creates Language" Zultanski
    who buys a Foster's Lager for
Steven "Passivity" Zultasnki
    who buys a Labatt Blue for
Steven "Free the Suffering Child" Zultanski
    who buys a Tecate for
Steven "Bearer of Simple Gifts" Zultanski
    who buys a Natural Light for
Steven "Mounting Paranoia" Zultanski
    who buys a Coors Light for

Steven "Incentive Mechanism" Zultanski
    who buys a New Belgium Fat Tire Amber Ale for
Steven "Rain Forest Metaphor" Zultanski
    who buys a Sea Dog Bluepaw for
Steven "Emergence of Art as a Human Social Function" Zultanski
    who buys a Russian Imperial Stout for
Steven "Raw Terror" Zultanski
    who buys a Widmer Hefeweizen for
Steven "Stricken with Facial Contortions" Zultanski
    who buys a Black Label for
Steven "The Receiving End" Zultanski
    who buys an Odoul's for
Steven "Self-Validation" Zultanski.

MAO!

Mao! You
look terrible in that painting with the tail in it.
In the fluctuating BMW, heavily-decaled, precipitating
the universal throttle of mind. Do you mean to throttle to
remain one?
Do you mean to accomplish secret thinking? Everyone else is
doing it,
and the abyss yawns from two sides. Mike, you're my best
friend.
You have always needed to be poor. I would give you a trumpet
if you could blow it, or that BMW with the tail in it,
blacked-out in the painting I made, the one by some ant-like
being
who didn't know anything, whose existence was suspected by no
one.
Mao! Dared to believe in the party of your dreams, the profane
image
as it descended like a spitball while you slept fitfully, smoldering
teen idol that you are. Mistook it for paintings by Mike,
mistook it for
custom helmet-paintings for your Porsche, Ferrari, or
motorcycle
in special effects colors. Metalflakes, chameleon pearls. You
protected
your "real me" preciously, almost maternally, to no particular
end.

I'm Picasso. I'm important. I'm soggy with intention.

A circular feeling bulges and recedes. Mao!
Mao awoke, and sat straight up in a beam of moonlight,
breathing heavy, expecting to be hauled away for her bath but
    instead
freshly childish as if she had already been returned. "I'm still
    alive?" She looked around.
She looked around. "I'm still alive?" Existence was shallow just
    then,
and the sponge of sadness soaked it up.
Mao! Daring to actually look into the envelope sent by a
    stranger,
the demands of entirely normal contradictions hovered like
    perfect sense, your
new love. A series of frustrating events eked out a Jupiter-sized
    depression, finally
secured by famine. With no trace of an object in the envelope, I
    hardly mattered.

Mike, you taught us how to love. Why do you go so quietly
into the office, so tired and old compared to your friends?
The path to the men's prison runs past. Perhaps you were
    walking
there. You used to do that elbow thing, and people
thought you were having sex. You used to do good things, full
    of spite,
a great artist pretending not to know how to paint a car with a
    tail in it,
and people thought you were having sex. Mao! The fruit of our
    laborious
communal life produces old nature, old hope. Spaces of wealth,

fantasy,

velvety-smooth chocolate indulgence. Spaces of unity won and
    kept

under precise experience, the accuracy of which materialism
    puts

never into doubt. Unless it is we don't survive. Unless the
    threat of death

glows in the dark, like great art, behind us. Unless the mind
    says "no,"

you cannot go beyond the visible. Unless, that is, the world is
    on fire,

and you have conclusive evidence that the contents of your
    address book

will lead you to the last unburnt family, unaware of the situation

until you materialize in their home, to everyone's surprise,

and explain to them their mistake.

Mao! Don't cry. The world isn't on fire all yet, and you don't
    look that bad.

Support is necessary, but streaks of turmoil organize
    revolutionary desire.

Mao! Look at this recluse spider and look at your hand wound.
    Make

the connection. Step from shadows, into the sun-bright beamer.

2.

Mike! You dork! I can't believe you shit in your boss's football
    helmet.
Murdering, prevented from looking at individuals, not
    answering the questions
someone without any stuff just asked – you shine into my
    farmer's hands.
I see little children enjoying the pleasure of stealing your waffles,
    beating you up,
and telling your parents. What will you eat? Mike! Lying in a
    dark retro diner
after hours, the broken window flushing in cold air, flaming
    snow
placenta lights in strobe the gruesome rhyme of your birth.
    Mao, you were
never born. The obedient cry does not rise. Parts of the body
    butchered
after a day's work, parts that don't heal, parts of the face. You
    visualize someone
coming to hit you, to attack your face. With hands held up to
    block
the view of the falling building, the scene seems bigger, more
    expansive,
like the blatant truth. I'll tell the little secret now. I'm going to
    hit you.

Mike! You look like a boy. When you take your shirt off, the
    laid back
and comfortable side of my personality gets bored, but my edgy
    and bumbling side
flutters. That's life. It dribbles away, insignificant and highly

descriptive.

This is Mao. This is a portrait of Mao.   Lushly I drizzle poems
    about fascinating

paintings, I dabble against dogmatism. Particularly, the
    bourgeoisie

are characterized by non-identity in the poem of the law

throttled by telekinesis. I, human mind, wait, gallantly ratting-
    out my own people,

freeing what industrial dust chokes half the world up, wedged
    between the sky.

Does bustedness incur change, or it is up to us to make
    abandoned city centers

rustle? A guess, at first minimalist, becomes enormous, before
    the subjective is transformed into the objective, and results
    are achieved in practice. Mike!

Towering naked in the bathroom, where we found a slow,

almost inert butterfly last night, I, contradiction, held your
    hand

while you ate a Cheerio lovingly offered by the saliva-covered
    fingers

of your nine-month old. Let me recreate that remembered
    feeling, and only

that feeling, exactly: when I was 16 I was caught stealing a
    burrito,

and when I was 18 I was caught burglarizing a drug store.

Now, at 22, I want to be a police officer, the way I want to be

on Jeopardy, the way the way has been made blindingly difficult
    at every step

by the stooges of the status quo, blasting car horns, obviously
    not

from this area. Mike! For no reason, I lied about dating a

younger boy,
because my mom would think I'm a loser. Mao lost his body
    and now he's stuck
in that cat's body. Maybe we'll see a flashback or something
to show how he actually lost his body, though he seems quite
    happy
in cat form, eating and sleeping all day. Mao, your
money is a mirror's old reflection. Nowhere is something else,
    entirely.

The inner swine whistles Dixie.

               The horizon was

        part,

axis. I announced that I would talk about the vulva. The
    organism
jumped on the furniture and wouldn't come down, curling up
    in neglect
of its wakefulness. Mao, you can see why these emoticons
    inhabit my speech, can't you?
For I feel nothing as I go, but know that others feel it for me.
    Others,
the social ones, extremes of saintliness and instinct, baffled by all
the examples that baffle us, governed by primordial function.
    Here is where
the organism, always on the point of collapsing, sits up, alert,
    and listens.
This is what I have to say. Alive with thought, sentimental,

Mike murders

the "me" of apology, the "me" of refusal and the "me" that is not
   for myself,

as well as the "I" of defense, the "I" of refusal and the "I" of
   sudden emergence.

Furthermore, I murder Mike. Mao! Hybrid rage of cloud and
   head,

your shadow gives gold to the intellectual course of the field.
   The peasants

and their beamers shine in gold. The form of virtue emboldens
   those at the margins

who see your painting-face shining. Mao! Why are you unsure
   of yourself, if you

are a cat? You look really dead. You look more fake than Lenin,

due to different embalming techniques, due to differences
   between countries

and the flowers contained therein. People decorate the graves of
   their own. The law

says so. Mao! Awakened, never to glance back, I am similar to
   flooded blue skies

churning around under a changed world. I am similar to me,
   hellishly. But you!

You look platitudinous, hope-ridden, turned into a happy
   mouse.

MAO'S MOMS

My mom helps Mao's mom
steal a loaf of bread
while Mao's Mom helps my
mom steal bags of rice
while my mom helps Mao's
mom steal a box of
crackers while Mao's mom helps
my mom steal a handful
of crispy prawn snacks while
my mom helps Mao's mom
steal a can of soup
while Mao's mom helps my
mom steal a bag of
broth while my mom helps
Mao's mom steal a box
of pasta while Mao's mom
helps my mom steal a
pack of instant noodles while
my mom helps Mao's mom
steal a flavored coffee while
Mao's mom helps my
mom steal a cup of tea.

Mao's mom helps my mom
steal a cup of tea
while my mom helps Mao's
mom steal a peach blossom
petal while Mao's mom helps

my mom steal a tree
peony petal while my mom
helps Mao's mom steal a
sunflower petal while Mao's mom
helps my mom steal a
China rose petal while my
mom helps Mao's mom steal
a prairie rose petal while
Mao's mom helps my mom
steal a lotus petal while
my mom helps Mao's mom
steal a panther lily petal
while Mao's mom helps my
mom steal a chrysanthemum petal
while my mom helps Mao's
mom steal a phlox petal.

My mom helps Mao's mom
steal a ten-gallon hat while
Mao's mom helps my mom
steal a conical bamboo hat
while my mom helps Mao's
mom steal a cotton bathrobe
while Mao's mom helps my
mom steal a silk robe
while my mom helps Mao's
mom steal a pin-striped three-piece
suit while Mao's mom helps
my mom steal a Mao
suit while my mom helps
Mao's mom steal a denim
mini-skirt while Mao's mom helps

my mom steal a cheongsam.

Mao's mom helps my mom
steal a Dongfeng Future while
my mom helps Mao's mom
steal a Chevrolet Suburban while
Mao's mom helps my mom
steal a Great Wall Wingle
while my mom helps Mao's
mom steal a Hummer while
Mao's mom helps my mom
steal a VW Passat Lingyu
while my mom helps Mao's
mom steal a VW Passat
while Mao's mom helps my
mom steal a Hongqi HQ3
while my mom helps Mao's
mom steal a Toyota Crown
while Mao's mom helps my
mom steal a Chery Tiggo
while my mom helps Mao's
mom steal a Ford Escort.

My mom helps Mao's mom
steal Frederick Edwin Church's "The
Heart of the Andes" while
Mao's mom helps my mom
steal Guo Xi's "Early Spring"
while my mom helps Mao's
mom steal Andy Warhol's "Mao"
while Mao's mom helps my
mom steal Zhang Zhenshi's "Portrait

of Mao" while my mom
helps Mao's mom steal an
"Uncle Sam Wants You" poster
while Mao's mom helps my
mom steal a "We will
crush the dog-heads of those
who oppose Chairman Mao" poster
while my mom helps Mao's
mom steal Robert Smithson's "Spiral
Jetty" while Mao's mom helps
my mom steal Cai Guo-Qiang's
"Project to Extend the Great
Wall of China by 10,000
Meters" while my mom helps
Mao's mom steal Tom Freidman's
"1,000 Hours of Staring" while
Mao's mom helps my mom
steal Song Dong's "Water Diary."

Mao's mom helps my mom
steal a door to the
Presidential Office Building while my
mom helps Mao's mom steal
a paint-chip from the White
House while Mao's mom helps
my mom steal a window
from the Shanghai World Financial
Center while my mom helps
Mao's mom steal a steel
beam out of the Empire
State Building while Mao's mom
helps my mom steal a

golden brick from the Forbidden
City while my mom helps
Mao's mom steal rolled barbed
wire from the Texas Border
Fence while Mao's mom helps
my mom steal the space
frame from the Bank of
China Tower while my mom
helps Mao's mom steal an
antennae from the Sears Tower
while Mao's mom helps my
mom steal a column from
the Tower of the Fragrance
of Buddha while my mom
helps Mao's mom steal the
capstone from the Washington Monument.

My mom helps Mao's mom
pull the head from an
ant while Mao's mom helps
my mom pull the pincers
from a beetle while my
mom helps Mao's mom
pull the soft hair from
a bumblebee while Mao's mom
helps my mom pull the
egg case from a cockroach
while my mom helps Mao's
mom pull the spinnerets from
a spider while Mao's mom
helps my mom pull the
compound eyes from a fly

while my mom helps Mao's
mom pull the venomous stinger
from a wasp while Mao's
mom helps my mom pull
all hundred legs from a
centipede while my mom helps
Mao's mom pull the scales
from a butterfly while Mao's
mom helps my mom pull
the wings from a cricket.

ALL MY WOMEN

All my Emily

All my Hannah

All my Madison

All my Ashley

All my Sarah

All my Alexis

All my Samantha

All my Jessica

All my Taylor

All my Elizabeth

All my Lauren

All my Kayla

All my Brianna

All my Emma

All my Grace

All my Alyssa

All my Abigail

All my Olivia

All my Megan

All my Victoria

All my Rachel

All my Sydney

All my Morgan

All my Haley

All my Nicole

All my Anna

All my Destiny

All my Jennifer

All my Jasmine

All my Julia

All my Kaitlyn

All my Natalie

All my Hailey

All my Stephanie

All my Savannah

All my Amanda

All my Katherine

All my Alexandra

All my Maria

All my Chloe

All my Rebecca

All my Mackenzie

All my Isabella

All my Mary

All my Gabrielle

All my Sophia

All my Allison

All my Amber

All my Danielle

All my Andrea

All my Jordan

All my Michelle

All my Katelyn

All my Kimberly

All my Courtney

All my Brooke

All my Sierra

All my Madeline

All my Sara

All my Erin

All my Brittany

All my Caroline

All my Jenna

All my Makayla

All my Paige

All my Vanessa

All my Jacqueline

All my Faith

All my Bailey

All my Shelby

All my Melissa

All my Christina

All my Caitlin

All my Marissa

All my Angela

All my Kaylee

All my Trinity

All my Mariah

All my Autumn

All my Zoe

All my Catherine

All my Laura

All my Jada

All my Alexa

All my Leslie

All my Breanna

All my Briana

All my Claire

All my Kelsey

All my Kathryn

All my Alexandria

All my Sabrina

All my Molly

All my Leah

All my Katie

All my Isabel

All my Mia

All my Gabriella

All my Cheyenne

All my Tiffany

COP KISSER

This little piggy loves to kiss my neck
and this little piggy loves to kiss in the rain
and this little piggy goes out of his way to kiss only lightly and
    call me Stevie
and this little piggy loves to kiss the hair on my legs
and this little piggy loves to kiss close so that our bellies rub
and this little piggy loves to kiss aggressively, pushing my lips
    back into my teeth until a little blood comes
and this little piggy loves to kiss my wounds
and this little piggy loves to kiss my scar
and this little piggy loves to kiss my likeness
and this little piggy loves to kiss my armpits and his moustache
    is so ticklish that I'm insane with laughter.

This little piggy goes to kiss my cheek but all the sudden his wet
    lips are on my wet lips and I doubt I'll be able enjoy the
    memory of this dream so decide to wake up
and this little piggy goes to kiss me but the steering wheel is in
    the way and when he tries to adjust it the horn gets stuck
and this little piggy goes to kiss me but ends up sort of biting
    me – which is even better, really, as I can talk about
    myself more profoundly if I'm experiencing a bit of pain
and this little piggy goes to kiss me but I turn, climb into the
    tub, turn on the tap and start moiling away at my
    privates with a sponge while she watches, handcuffs
    dangling like parachute pull cords that I keep pulling
    and pulling but no parachute comes

and this little piggy goes to kiss me like he used to, far too
    formally and not at all beckoning the presence of our
    future casual encounters
and this little piggy kisses me there and there where I'm caught
    in the in-between
and this little piggy goes to kiss me but instead pins me to a wall
and this little piggy goes to kiss me the way one would kiss a
    baby, on the soft top of the head, and I bow a little
    forward to let him in, to meet his gentleness,
    momentarily experiencing someone else's desire not
    as something abstract and readily terrible but as the
    simple difference between me and my generosity
and this little piggy goes to kiss me with a beard kept soft
    through thrice-daily conditioning rinses
and this little piggy goes to kiss me and I see his large open
    mouth expand and scream as he swallows us whole.

I.

                    A cop is a cop
                     is a cop
                    is shooting
                     out
                    of his finger and
                     touching the tip
                    of his little pink nose
                     tickling
                    like a glitch
                     from crossed wires or speech aphasia
                    from a cop
                     shooting out another

bodily sensation
   of another finger
that brushes my nipple
   like the concept
of pain inverted as
   a cop
does not project beyond the free edge
   of the brushed body
which shoots
   a bird
which flutters past
   like a finger
at my lips
   across which
as any young traveler who has seen the
beach
   knows about the waves
they shoot foam
   out of their fingers
just as a cop
   shoots a wine glass
full of wine
   and I shatter like a lovesick puppy
dog
showered in
   kisses
and eye-rolls
   and sheer
and obvious
   generosity
shooting smoothest
   silk

from his finger
   as it touches the tip
of my tongue
   waggling
secret birdsongs
   to a blushing
weak state
   to put
lipstick on
   my little piggy
in pensiveness
   muscular
and long flowing hair we have
   so
   we have
      so
similar first names and our birthdays
      are the same
and this little piggy
   strokes my hair and
moves my arms
   so that I sort of
hold myself as a baby and caress myself
      and cry helplessly
   as a cop's
      tender
wrestling show is on with eyes so wide
   and getting so much
wider
   in his sleep
of a permanent similarity to the
   blinding light

                    of a cop's
                  white
                      eyes
                  shooting invisible beams of heat at
                    a sweetheart
                  in the leg
                      to make him
                  speak up and say
                      his sweetest
                  things
                      as a thing is
                  in his own ear.

Hug the police. Truly
they want to enter on our side and exit
the other side of the finger. They
are them, and them's the rules,
the curved human kinds of dangerous poo resolved
into normal political source code, the formal
portability of introduced order presenting the back of
the other side of the finger. You either have it,
or you don't – a future. Familiar enough obstructions, like walls
    on top of walls
walk the streets, doling out behavior in excess of love, washing
ashore all manner of accident, from face to face to
most tender lullaby. I, Stevie,
sing to you if you will hear me out of myself, coming totally as a
    promise
to hear you in return, my funny one, my very funny one.
Little piggy, I want you to look at me
so I bought you this pair of underwear and stuffed myself in

at least half as much as you can love me, with or without
my best intentions being more a relative function of priorities
and less a secret to be kept or laid bare. Arrest yourself already
for being on
the other side of the finger.

The other side of the finger sleeps.
It dreams of a dream job that doesn't yet exist yet punches out
through the wall of the home and into the percussive time-space
that we barely understand as day to day to
broken down day. Work is still work. The maximum
     punishment
is life. The police break up
and go their separate way, only to reform
as larger blobs with complete mastery of all matter,
wholly indebted to nothing
but the fortuitous confluence of verges
that allowed them to break up
in the first place, and to a lesser extent to introduce objects into
     our empty midst,
like jelly. I drop to the floor their memories,
miserable to the core and mostly involving a headless
version of my infant self in fetal position, playing dead
too lifelessly to fake pain. Sirens don't wail,
they ding-dong. They
are them, hanging the door that they knock on.

and this little piggy holds me from behind and leans in to kiss
     me on both shoulders
and this little piggy holds me from behind and kisses with so

much tongue that he licks my face nearly off

and this little piggy holds me from behind and rests her nose in
    my hair

and this little piggy holds me from behind and nibbles my ears

and this little piggy holds me from behind and kisses my chest
    and ribs and stomach and then I'm in his mouth

and this little piggy holds me from behind and reminds me of
    just how incomplete I am

and this little piggy holds me from behind and sings loudly and
    unwaveringly in-key about this same foundational
    incompleteness

and this little piggy holds me from behind, stares into the
    bathroom mirror and watches herself kiss my bare back

and this little piggy won't stop kissing the soap from my skin as
    I shiver

and this little piggy holds me from behind and rubs a washcloth
    over the bruises covering my body.

but what really burns my cookies, the thing
that makes me want to come back from the dead
    to tell you all my story of unwritten kisses
as well as the tale of his curly tail wrapped around my
    pinky finger
        like a wedding ring
            in the middle of a
    wedding bed
is this little piggy won't stop kissing my face even though

I

just

put
on
gooey,
glittery,
passionfruit-flavored
lip
gloss
and
she
won't
stop
kissing
my
boots.

PERSONAGES

Inuit families
give their
children
away, but
the Qashqui
nomads
make
colorful saddlebags
superior
to all
others. Russians
consider
gold a luxury.
The French are cold.
Afghani men kiss
their babies'
genitals.
It is a
traditional
expression of
love, but
Cambodian
parents place
hot objects
on their children's
foreheads during
illness,

and the
family
of a Welsh
bride
steals
her from her
wedding
as
the groom's
family
madly
pursues.

Roman husbands
kissed their wives
on the mouth,
but not
in a romantic way.
Laplanders
rub noses together.
Polynesians
do too.
A kiss in Samoa
is a sniff in the air.
The breaking
of the glass
is a reminder
of the destruction
of the temple
in Jerusalem, and many
native people
in Peru think

of the soul as
birdlike. It flies
from the sleeping
body
and returns
upon awakening.
For Buddhists,
funerals are happy
occasions.
Subsidized bread.

What's
this
morality
play
about?
Mostly
about
fear.
I'm
an
artist
because
it's
one
of
the
few
things
you
can
do

in
this
country
that
has
no
rules,   .

but the Vietnamese
leaf-covered
conical hat
is unique
among
Asia's conical
hats. It is
called
"Poetical Leaf."
Australians
offer food
and drink only
once.
Ethiopians
don't use
utensils. They
like it when their kids
are smart.
In
Indonesia,
one might grow
a long fingernail
as
tissue paper. In

Thailand
the foot is held
in low esteem –
it is the lowest
part of the body,
and greetings
in Asia
consist of a bow.
A crooked finger
in Japan is obscene,
but there are timed
parking meters
for bicycles.
Indians smash
a certain kind of
vegetable
to ward off evil spirits.

I've
seen
cows,
oxen,
buffalo,
goats,
dogs
and
even
pigs
wandering
the
streets.
But

I've

yet

to

see

a

single

cat.

I'm told that cats
are
inauspicious
animals.
There have
been several
examples of
this view
throughout
history. Plato
wrote that art
should display
socially
acceptable,
responsible
messages. In
the 50s,
rice was thrown
at a wedding.
I remember chickens
pecking at my
ankles
when I was
a little

girl in
Poland.

Whatever
is
contrary
to
established
manners
and
customs
is
immoral.
An
immoral
act
or
doctrine
is
not
necessarily
a
sinful
one:
it
is
of
the
most
enormous
importance
that

immorality
should
be
protected
jealously
against
those
who
have
no
standard
except
the
standard
of
custom,

and Italians
find it important
to acknowledge
the presence of
another
person. Canada's
public parks
and buildings
are lit for the
holidays, all
lit at once.

You
think
it

is
like
everything
else,
a
sort
of
game.

The
Mound-Builders
wrap
the body
in
bark. In Ohio
and West Virginia
mounds, a
layer of bark
is placed on
the bottom
of
the grave.
Korean men
walk with
their arms around
each other's
shoulders, and
teenage girls
walk hand in
hand. Icelanders
are generally reserved
and confident,

though sometimes
wary
of foreigners. The
Irish carry rabbits'
feet because
they
believe
rabbits are lucky.
The Irish have
a bad view
of cats.
After every sip
of drink
taken,
wipe your mouth
in Brazil. Food
should always
be shared, even
if the amount
of food
is clearly not
sufficient
to share.

A
story.
An
interesting
fact.

It is "good form"
for a host

to accompany
his Arab
visitor
to the street
or waiting
car, but Afghanis
distribute
green onions
during the song
"Deyenu."

    Beginning
    with
    the
    stanza,
    "Even
    if
    you
    supplied
    our
    needs
    in
    the
    desert
    for
    forty
    years,
    and
    not
    fed
    us
    manna

from
heaven,"

the participants
hit each other
with the green
onion stalks, every
time
they sing
the refrain. There
is a very strange
ritual in America
that happens
every four years.
Hair snakes.
Men cover their arms
and legs in
Syria, and women
cover their heads,
but who
kisses the hands
of the
elderly?

The
artist
must
conform
to
the
current.

Spaniards eat
lunch
between 2:00
and 4:00 in the
afternoon. New
Chinese mothers
go through a
mandatory
confinement period
to drive the
wind
of childbirth
from
their bodies. Spiritual
wind. The Dutch
do not touch
each other or
display extreme
exuberance,
but in my area
it's slutty
for the girl
to ask the guy
out. The Massai
avoid killing cows,
preferring to use
products
yielded by the
animal
while it is alive.

A

piñata
is
a
decorated
container
filled
with
candies.
The
container
can
be
any
shape.
Examples
are
a
donkey
or
a
star.

Oral traditions are
safeguarded.
Forty-one percent
of French adults
have participated
in an orgy, but
seven times a
year,
Indonesians
spend a night

having sex
with someone
other
than their spouse,
on a sacred
mountain on
Java. Egyptian
men stay home
and weave. In
Iraq, the soles
of your shoes
should not point
at anyone.

    They
    recently
    claimed
    that
    the
    airport
    x-rays
    do
    not
    harm
    film,

but typical Cuban
cuisine
makes use of pork,
fowl, rice
and tropical fruit.

I
cannot
hug
my
neighbor.

In Japanese,
the word for
"house"
can also mean
"person." The
Sioux language
has no word
for "late" or
"waiting." Mandarin
has no equivalent
to "the."
A Chinese
expression
of thanks means,
"I have
caused you
some trouble." To
give someone
a "rough time"
in French
is to make
make someone
go through a
"rough 15 minutes."

Is

morality
about
who
we
are
or
what
we
do?
Is
it
the
theme
of
some
of
Freidrich
Neitzsche's
works?

For some
Island folk,
carrying bat bones
is lucky, but killing
bats is bad luck.
Greek women
spit thrice on
their
cleavage to ward
off misfortune.

Dark

coffee.

Amulets.

In Italy
they
have no Christmas
trees.
Venezuelans
roller-skate to
church
on Christmas eve.
Ukranians include
artificial spiders
and webs on
their Christmas
trees, but the
English make
a wish
while mixing
pudding
clockwise.
Solstice
brings the longest
day. On
the island of
Chiloé, it
is common to
move entire
houses on
tree trunks
drawn by

oxen, and
Romanians
clean
their houses
thoroughly
before Easter.
Hungarians
invented BASIC
programming language
and the theoretical
background
of the hydrogen
bomb.
Another old
Swiss tradition
is the right
of sanctuary,
and according to
an international poll,
France is the
only country, among
twenty, where
the majority of
people said "no"
to the question,
"Do you think
that the system of
free enterprise
and market economy
is best
for the future?"

The
evil
eye
can
strike
at
any
given
moment.

Eggs are
dyed red
to symbolize
the blood of Christ.
Our wines
do not sell as well
as they used to.
You can judge
the artist
from the perspective
of morality,
and in Kashmir
the eating of stale food
is prohibited.
Detroit hockey fans
throw an octopus
on the ice.
I confess,

I
want
Latin.

Do you know
about any
movies
with really
weird
aliens?

A
child
holds
a
hard-boiled
egg
as
an
adult
throws
a
coin
at
the
egg
in
an
attempt
to
pierce
the
shell
and
wedge

the
coin
in
the
egg.

An immortal
little bone
at the bottom
of its
ascetic origins.

Vatican
City's
security
is
guaranteed
by
the
Swiss
Guard.
Bathing-suited
participants
bathe
in
snow
in
temperatures
of
- 20°
before
returning

to
saunas
to
warm
up.
In
Kashmir
there
is
a
legend
that
Jesus
did
not
die
on
the
cross.
They
even
point
to
his
grave.

In ancient Israel,
people
put
the sins of
the nation
onto a goat

and sent the
goat
into the desert.
The Nepalese
do not work
on full moon
or new
moon days,
and among
the Rais,
marriages
are monogamous,
but ordinary
mortals
are not permitted
to go
near the river.

There
is
no
obvious
moral
or
logical
reason
for
this
tradition.

Cow-fighting
is popular

in the
Valais – true
or false?
Have you ever
seen strange
people? They appear
out of nowhere,
pass you by.
When you
look back, there's
no one there.

Ideas
can
be
crushed,
and
I,

stranger
in a strange
city. Prisoner
of immobility.
The inhabitants
of Holzkirchen
carry a
heavy candle
up a hill every
spring. Thais
smile for all
occasions.
Church bells

announce
a death throughout
the villages
of Portugal,
and the house
of the deceased
is opened so
that people may
enter and join
the family in
mourning,
and in Burma
there are no
family
names or surnames.

What
are
the
facts
that
give
rise
to
the
concept
of
marriage,

and why
do people
vow

to love one
another
when they
wed? Moral
tradition
is the continuing
transmission
and reception
of
related moral
themes
through multiple
generations.

Finger
snapping.

The Chinese
do not like to do
business
with strangers. Do
not use the word
"comrade"
in China. At
Hawai'i weddings,
the bride and
groom do a
money dance, and
Uganda's government
distributes
portraits of
their

president.
The French are rude.
An old
Argentinian tradition
in
neurobiology
focuses on
neurobiophysics and
phylogeny. A
knot.
Celebrating
family.
Danes
throw rice.
In Chile,
dead children
are dressed
in white
and given
paper wings
before burial.
A
Congolese
therapist will treat
asthma with
crayfish, because
crayfish contains
the water
genie
that drives witches
away,
but

when a Turkish
boy gets circumcised,
everyone in
attendance
drives through
town

honking
their
horns.

Elder and
prominent
Ethiopians
knock on families'
doors
early in the
morning to
bear news
of death
in
war.

Slovenian-style
polka
is
an
American
style
of
polka
in

the
Slovenian
tradition.

But Koreans
give the gift
of
wedding ducks
at a wedding. Sometimes
the female
duck's beak
is tied
shut
with a
ribbon.
In Ghana,
the dead are buried
in elaborate "fantasy
coffins"
that come
carved in everything
from airplane
to fish styles.

I
have
no
idea
why
people
sit
on

the
floor
or
take
the
TV
out
of
the
living
room.

Olive oil
is not a
historical element
of Malta,
but female
genital cutting
is a deeply
rooted practice
in some
Kenyan tribes,
and Serbs
offer
their guests
something
sweet to drink.
Canadians ice-fish.
Jerk
spice.

The

total
suppression
of
immorality
would
stop
enlightenment.
The
dead
weight
of
human
inertia
hangs
on
the
artist's
back.
He
must
be
original,
courageous,
inspiring,
and
all
that.
I,

artist,

stop

enlightenment.

Iranians wear
wide belts with
decorative
metal plaques,
and the Chinese
don't
wash their hair
on the new
year.
The French are passionate.

People
don't
applaud
after
a
performance.

POEM FOR DICK BUTKUS

I never knew John Wayne

_____

but I did meet Dick Butkus.

Heroes: Dick Butkus, My parents, Julius Caesar, Jesus Christ, John Elway, Joesph Smith, Jerry Seinfeld, Chuck Norris, James Bond.

Dick Butkus: The Man Behind College Football's Dick Butkus
Award

I was so

_____

excited

_____

about football

_____

that I needed

_____

a hero.

Besides

———————————

Dick Butkus

———————————

who would you

———————————

least like

———————————

to hit you?

Dick Butkus and
the Orange County Heart Institute

———————————

———————————

join forces
to prevent steroid abuse.

Who I'd like to meet: Bill Clinton, Dick Butkus, my dad when he was in his 20's, Mark Twain, Johnny Depp, FDR, Marilyn Monroe, Ghandi, Charlie Chaplin, Harry Carey, Benny Hill.

But Dick Butkus, who once said his goal was to hit someone so hard that the man's head came off,

At The Dick Butkus Fan Shop

_____

Browse Our Dick Butkus Shop

_____

& Get Ready For The Big Dick Butkus

_____

Game

Heroes: My sons Aidan and Gunnar, my grandparents, Benjamin Franklin, President Ronald Reagan, Dick Butkus, the Marines who fought at Belleau Wood, the Marines who fought on Iwo Jima, the Marines who fought on Tarawa and all the men and women who have served in our great nation's military services to protect our way of life.

Then Butkus said,
'Hey, I'm Dick Butkus
and I give out
  this thing

_____

called the Butkus Award.'

Who I'd like to meet: Pope Benedict XVI, Senator John McCain, Dick Butkus, Chuck Norris, General Norman Schwartzkopf, Steven Seagal.

Dick Butkus
loves

_____

his uncle.

Who I'd like to meet: Myself in 40 years, Rob Zombie, Michael Jordan, Dick Butkus, my parents 30 years ago.

Is it true

_____

that if I rub
butter on my breasts

_____

they will grow?

I don't know

———————————

if I need to kiss butt to

———————————

get good sushi.

I refuse

_____

to kiss butt for someone who expects you to kiss butt

_____

on a daily basis.

Related topics: dog, dogs, ambition, ambitions, excessive ambition, excessive ambitions, boot-licking, boot-licker, boot-lickers, butt-kissing, butt-kisser, butt-kissers, suck up, sucking up, sycophant, sycophants, therapy, psychiatry, psychology, counseling,

Have the kids

_____

rub butter

_____

on their hands.

Kiss the

_____

blues

_____

goodbye.

I'm Dick Butkus.

_____

I'm a little

_____

butt.

All that pent-up frustration,

_____

_____

as I patrolled the trenches like Dobermans.

Dick Butkus climbed on the bed

_____

next to Dick Butkus

_____

quietly.

Never rub butter
on your cat's paws

———————————

so it can smell the way home.

———————————

All you'll get
is a greasy cat.

ME AND MY BROTHER PEE ON EACH OTHER

My brother pees on my Almond Joy Bar

so

I pee on his Butterfinger Bar

so

he pees on my Chunky Bar

so

I pee on his Dove Bar

so

he pees on my E. Guittard Semisweet Chocolate Bar

so

I pee on his Fifth Avenue Bar

so

he pees on my Good News Bar

so

I pee on his Heath Bar

so

he pees on my Idaho Spud Bar

so

I pee on his Jolly Rancher Stick

so

he pees on my Kit Kat Bar

so

I pee on his Look Bar

so

he pees on my Mars Bar

so

I pee on his Milky Way Bar

so

he pees on my Moose Munch Bar

so

I pee on his Mounds Bar

so

he pees on my Mountain Bar

so

I pee on his Mr. Goodbar Bar

so

he pees on my Munch Nut Bar

so

I pee on his Nestle Crunch Bar

so

he pees on my Oh Henry Bar

so

I pee on his Payday Bar

so

he pees on my Q.bel Peanut Butter Wafer Bar

so

I pee on his Rocky Road Bar

so

he pees on my Snickers Bar

so

I pee on his Twix Bar

so

he pees on my U-No Bar

so

I pee on his Violet Crumble Bar

so

he pees on my Whatchamacallit Bar

so

I pee on his Xploder Bar

so

he pees on my Yorkie Bar

so

I pee on his Zero Bar.

MY BEST POEM

I love you, Officer Dick Buttanski, because you make me
obsessively
ever-present
to myself,
as my mom.

I love you, Officer Shitty Jerktanski, because just hearing
your breath
in my mouth
makes me
regret literacy.

I love it when you
call me names,
and the implied meanings
of said names
suddenly emerge as
my most
characteristic features.

For example,
Officer Idiot Fooltanski.

Or,
Officer Bumbly Clutztanski.

I love you, Officer Dweeb Puketanski, because you make me
see
skin color
as a form
of genitalia.

But at least I'm happier
than about 85%
of the people I know.

LENIN MINUS ONE

Lenin shoots a large fiery skull
out of his mouth

Lenin shoots water
out of his mouth

Lenin shoots the teeth of a neighing horse
out of his mouth

Lenin shoots white lights
out of his mouth

   *

Just the other day
I was in Future Shop,

paying $50
for an ink cartridge

and wishing for that moment
that Canada was communist.

   *

Lenin shoots candy
out of his mouth

Lenin shoots a ring of lasers
out of his mouth

*

I hate paying
for gas.

I hate paying
for food.

I hate paying
for water.

I have a wireless
mouse

but I use my mouse
with a cord because

I hate paying
for batteries.

*

I hate paying for street lights
in neighborhoods in which

I don't live.
I need the car

so I can go places.

It's time for a beer.

*

Lenin shoots a dark-skinned Asiatic Indian-looking woman
out of his mouth

Lenin shoots a spiky ball
out of his mouth

Lenin shoots a jetstream of hellfire
out of his mouth

Lenin shoots a beer
out of his mouth

*

Bottled water:
my only option.

*

Lenin shoots black moss
out of his mouth

Lenin shoots his unconscious
out of his mouth

*

This

drags on.

The experience of the individual
alone

occupies
the grey barracks

of its dreamscapades.
People stalk

stores.
Cockroaches

crawl out
of the mouths of

policemen.
It is day.

*

It is day –
with vengeances.

*

I hate paying
for ammo

when I don't
use it.

Just the other day
I was in Home Depot

looking for something
to plant in the yard.

*

Lenin shoots ice balls
out of his mouth

Lenin shoots protein
out of his mouth

Lenin shoots two pencil-thin three-inch blades
out of his mouth

Lenin shoots rainbows
out of his mouth

*

Lenin shoots a mass of energy
out of his mouth

*

Your umbrella
cannot protect you

from Lenin's rainbows.

148

Unfinished, the course of events

blows through

our embossed
K-style gutters.

    *

Fuming plants
where those they work.

    *

Lenin shoots steam
out of his mouth

Lenin shoots a ripping noise
out of his mouth

Lenin shoots a phoenix made of earth
out of his mouth

    *

Lenin's glass-shattering scream pierces the hearts
of the worker-bees. A hulking leviathan emboldened
by the sight of a pretty snazzy genderless stereotype,
Lenin swings into the dark recesses of the demands of history,
along the wall, in the shadow of the wall. It
is clear and casts a fresh light on the absolute
requirements of being in the shadow, the lack of the lack

of killing, the shadow childishly determining
who does the killing but never whom is being killed.
Calculations make you soft. She approaches as a sufferer
shooting mounds out of her mouth. With a migraine

C-cup

the pros and cons cry, wishing that their fathers were hostile.
Their fathers were not hostile but horrible, harboring beliefs as
     they did
of thrift as a virtue, of saving up as perhaps the final form
of responsibility in a culture obsessed with dissembling
the goofs of rainmaking excess. Semi-unwillingly, but for fun, I
     collect
racist objects, to teach kids an incriminatory tolerance
modeled on an ethics of professional courtesy. Painting
the lawn jockey white. Playing the tenor sax.
Fuck white people for being Buddhists. Don't you have a cop
to kill? You don't know what a butt's for?
Your hips are the hips of the masses,
indifferent to the thousand pages of labor history
a dude laid down in a novel, just for you and your special
     friends.
Lenin shoots rays of sunshine out of his mouth.

Lenin shoots jewel after jewel out of his mouth.

Lenin's ten-year-old-son's head shoots out of his mouth and

laughs at her.

Your roving death squad or mine? We are thankful
for such frankness involuted by realism, the narrative
retooled to illuminate the reaches of memory. It allows us
to mimic life in all its shades and hues of cockroach,
to make a motion:
Being a good boy is no harder than being
a bad boy insofar as both kinds are born with the assholes
of our same horrible fathers' vacancies. Such sneaky
    presuppositions
creep our citizens out. Like peeling off the slinky hormonal
bodystocking to reveal a mash of woodies. Until then
                  yeah, fine, I will refer
to this benchmark era as end over end, but I'll come back
    tomorrow
as heir of nightmares. One archaic characteristic, sunlight,
    sweetens the day
when it is day, turns it into night, the silent expression of busy
    distant
worker-beetles burning energy, smoked gouda on top of each
    piece of meat.

*

Just the other day I was thinking
about a touchscreen phone

but not the iPhone.
You can brainwash me all you want,

but I will not think

about the iPhone.

*

The Mogul is the most robust
handset

and when I think of robust I think
of a phone

that can utilize the most
features.

*

If someone with authority
is confronted

by someone else with authority
they heed

Democracy is the best
method

ever

*

Ever

*

Lenin muttered
  I don't have any stirrups
dryly through his teeth.

Despite incomparable power

I want a new job
driving

The Wienermobile

*

Lenin shoots public money
out of his mouth

Lenin shoots red lines
out of his mouth

Lenin shoots hypnotic emerald beams
out of his mouth

*

I hate paying for beer
without a head

but I really hate paying for stuff
that I can't touch

but I really hate paying for car repairs
especially tires

but I really hate paying for music

I hate the smell of ovens

but I really hate paying for food
because there's no way out of it

*

Deep

bunk.

*

I hate paying for that
from which
I receive no benefit.
Like Congress.

*

Lenin's phone is ringing. The oppressor is calling. I want to
    realize
revolution but non-intentionally, escape-pod-esque, when there
    is
no further desire by anyone for anything but a new day, because
    the lights

have gone dark and the food mildly stale. Inevitably, like a
   human face,
he can be seen. Lenin shoots a targeting reticule out of his
   mouth
and paints a spot on the ground where rockets land. I want to
   realize
the ever-changing disallowment. Then the rigid gist. Then the
   dulled huddle.
She felt the vague sensation
of an inability to do a back-flip to get away.
You earn what you're worth – needless work. You earn

   points. But if you like coins

Forever grateful to the police for their touches, seamless
and unsuited for chaos, lies or occupation – Lenin would not
tolerate flowers in his room. Not for an instant, not a wobble.
Taking our cue from the effective doubt that merely appears
all-encompassing, our aims go against the aims of the innocent
and pious lone truth, spiritual experience mistaken for personal
criticism. But mistaken by whom? The environment? The most
   rational solution

the leggiest

on the coast or in the jungle, the most beautiful of all modernist
spiral stairs. Faith in pre-Armageddic social contracts is not
   entirely
reactionary. Faith in Armageddon, however, is.

Existing theories lurk, lover-like, in my complete and sonorous
impressions, which provide me with inutile enjoyment, banal

observations elevated to the ranks of reverie – look, an army,
     look, a rose
put under a circular archway. I am looking for the shadow of
     my double,
the formula for a necessary social bond where there is none.
A generic trumpet call brings me back
to the brink of wakefulness, but I recognize nothing and
     accomplish
no dreams, nothing beyond experience
to speak of but a few catchy tunes.

Lenin is ready still. He calls for immediate counter-armistice.
     To repudiate
secret treaties by which we have been bound up to the present
     time,
trapping us in an office instead of on top of Mt. Everest
     looking out over Wall Street,
pointing always toward the breast of the advancing enemy
     already
advanced, on top of us, pushing him off, arms outstretched
to the counterperson, exchanging coins and dollars for peace,
     bread, and freedom.

                    *

Lenin shoots daggers
out of his mouth

Lenin shoots webs
out of his mouth

Lenin shoots a sonic fence

out of his mouth

Lenin shoots a radioactive blast
out of his mouth

Lenin shoots mirrors
out of his mouth

Lenin shoots a starburst of cosmic sound
out of his mouth

Lenin shoots a jet of venom
out of his mouth

Lenin shoots some days
out of his mouth

Lenin shoots five or six pearly diamonds
out of his mouth

Lenin shoots anvils
out of his mouth

Lenin shoots sparks
out of his mouth

Lenin says, "Those are
parabeams!"

Parabeams shoot
out of his mouth

Lenin shoots a frothy gel of white cream
out of his mouth

Lenin shoots herself
out of his mouth

He bites into an apple.

Lenin shoots his double
out of his mouth

Lenin shoots experimental life
out of his mouth

HELL

1.

The mighty worlds are full of hell.
Full of bosses and the echoes
of their orders, clashing harshly
with the unappeasable desire
for violence. They
are them. They support the dreaminess
of the good men and bad men,
those who feel at the outset ousted,
kissed into sexual prematurity
by a stranger who had the full joy of life
in him

but couldn't get it out.

Hell is near insofar as it is a ways off
but always in sight, like a really tall
office building on the horizon as you step
and take a step back. I take off a day, or a week.
I understand that all of my worldly pleasures
are predicated on the immiseration of peoples,
and I have nothing but worldly pleasures, nothing
outside of the world. War is just a part of hell.
The entire immiseration of peoples is hell.

Come, violence.
I don't want you

to think you're special, but you are the only thing
for no good reason, the pervasive half-assedness
of the puny human present. Only a fucking fuck-face
would disagree. Only a face-fucking capitalist could prove
    otherwise

using science, math or reason. But I can do otherwise
by playing a relentless game
of hide-and-seek involving several
theoretical hiding spots that remain simply unfindable
due to their non-existence and/or exceptionally small size.
I can also play hard-to-get. I can also go to hell.

Hell is what you get
when you put two and two together.
There the distinctions between people are specific,
not private. Freedom has great value,
        i.e. no specific
value. It's not measured in terms of pitch, but in lack
of capacity, the anti-utilization of a potential skill-set,
the lazy summer day spent inside
a basic form of decency and goodness
instead of sucked in the rigidity of daily working hours,
        i.e. a separate
self independent of expectations, a self
without feet to prop on the boss's desk.

2.

Difference is hell. Despite the dangers, there is the staying
there. Until you respawn you will zoom in and out,
forever trying to find the perfect setting for your snuff film,

the one you've been making about yourself, starring
the sad reality
                    that no one is forced to accept.
In that movie, dogs bite at your heels and ankles
like a darker, more gory version of 101 Dalmatians
in which you move away from zero, but find no path
to the other side of zero, to anything resembling a one.
Hell is different from nudity, it doesn't reveal what seems at first as a truth –
in it a minute isn't another.

My boss is nuts.

I make copies.
I'm unembarrassed by my finite form.
It's hell to be a continual rolling
of stones upon dead bodies.
It's hell to be caught in the promises of history
and instead writing copy.

                Each boss assumes
                no chance of a world
                without hell. One by one they've
                seen nothing to suggest that the planet
                has been inhabited and altered by living creatures
                there. Remotely similar in no meaningful way
                are the identical sexes who recently had or had not
                fallen in love or were "just friends." I've
                seen nothing to suggest the presence of women.
                Each boss assumes the identity
                of a single person, and sometimes a single
                boss assumes the identity of many,

if he or she can eliminate the duration of man
i.e. no second
sole survivor. They
are them, and then they beat us back.

Demons take over the planet! Exclamation point.
Bodies with a singular head and the wings of birds
swarm in opposite directions. The swarm holds
together. It brings us to our male and female knees,
like the rubble of a building that has not yet completely
    collapsed,
the zero-sum game that someone just won.
I have also been shattered, like everything else
by the pain of childbirth, the guarantee
that life goes on, and so on –
even when there's no more on and on,
when the skin has literally grown around the toilet seat
and the approval of others decays into the addiction
to food. I also decay too. I disintegrate
and reform as an anger going wholly undivided,
as a piece of hell as solid and real as a park bench
in a sunny park on a lazy summer day spent sunning
full of hell, hell and hell! Exclamation point.

3.

Introductions will continue until each person
has eaten his crackers, and each person will continue
to eat his crackers for all of eternity, and that is hell
too.

4.

Ever since my brain problem,
I've been living life to the fullest.
Each morning I walk down
to the Institute for Social Research
by climbing and descending a hill
that used to run with hot springs, no longer
in evidence but not so distant so as to be forgotten
by us locals, ever present to the greenery.
I wax nostalgic
with my friends and say to them:
"I wish I could go somewhere where
my me-time is not despised," but where else
is there to go in hell?
Well then, to a little end unit
across the street from Wall Street,
where remorse was first felt by time itself,
but no remorse is longer felt by me for now
since I've been significantly forced, by will or fate,
to contemplate certain seemingly random alignments
of letters
and to finger myself out as an idiot
one after another in their presence.

So why then am I lurking in the lobby
of the school of management?
I am looking for a protégé.

You there! You approached me as a second thought,
an individual,
and as the same person

who had an experience in the past
as I have.
I returned to this past without you, only to find you've been
had
by a paralysis of nerve-shattering inaction,
and then that I had you too, at the very least as content.

All the best
stuff
is hellish, because
hell is phenomenal, and so is pain.
The business of business remains to be seen,
like a pocket deep in his or her robes –

the clumsy grossness of the hole in the human creature,
the ordinary man at the peak of his aristocracy.

5.

Naturally,
the country that exports capital
skims the cream.

If ever there was a good thing,
then this isn't it
because this isn't real –
            it's a thought-experiment.
Picture this: a hole in one.

Hell is being on the green,
and hell is being kept off the green: this is the paradox
of hell.

Picture this: farting
on a JPEG:

Squeezing the white sand
between your fingers:

Stuck in the
pit:

Trapped in there without the big question on hand, in the gun
    shop
where I met your beast of a mother in all my weaknesses
like elements in an affective chain, each approximately
    individual
but produced only in their constitutive movement. We escaped
through China, making our way out the door we came in to,
young and in love and sharing our dream of a life together for
a lot of eternity. Good times. The most disorienting experience
of the day came early on and the rest was just a series of side
    effects.
I used the voice of a boy to cover my lack of confidence,
and the sound was like something you might have wanted
to hear if you were listening for an actual word.
                    The first time you heard it
you imagined yourself as the invisible guest of the baron,
watching the sunset from his balcony. But later on,
in a perfectly quiet room, you imagined instead of opening one
sandwich shop, starting a chain of sandwich shops
throughout the city, where the employees could wear
their Hawaiian shirts and plastic gloves freely. Finally, a place
just for you
but without you there.

So, I got your dream tattoo, the one I always wanted you to
    want, in memory of your wanting it.
And then I paid a little extra rent this month, just to show up
    the landlord.

It's hard to bottom out when the bottom
is everywhere. Rubbing, stubborn,

passionately giving each other hugs all the time.
Our sex life has suffered, but our friendship has grown.
My friends, I would like to deliver to you this prize, in the form
    of
a strong emotion. Take this hug. It is a symbol of that very
    same
strong emotion which you already show. You might deserve to
    rest,
but there is still work to do before you can afford to pay off
the traffic fines. For now, the rich get to win the consolation
    prize of being rich,
and as for the rest of us, we get to understand that we will never
    know
our neighbors, but instead, as if there were another kind of
consolation, we will continue to mull over the concrete
details of their absolutely satisfying motherfucking hours. The
    rest does not apply.

The rich are only defeated
when running for their lives.

6.

There's a thousand
yous.
There's only one
of me.

I take this to be
axiomatic.

The straight-up banality
of insight throws light onto that which had previously appeared
to be throwing light, but is clearly throwing something merely
    approximate
to light. Such is a shadow, the direct result
of a plausible future in which I am never new
and the president slips on a banana peel.
Did I eat the delicious banana? Yes,
I hope so, but that doesn't mean I thought far enough ahead
to drop the peel.
I myself remained
inside the lines, and the lines themselves were long.

Unimpressive as I am as a person, I'm distinct enough
if you think of me as a predicament. Before creation,
there must have been only one age. Now I grow older right
    away.
But at least it's always a new kind of old, and each new kind is
    immediately
overpowered by the different sides of the brain which drive
me out. Home is where what I think of as my heart is.
A cold, fully-automated cafeteria in the basement of a hotel.

The only place I've ever felt alone enough to engage in this
        activity
which we refer to as explicitly sexual is here, and the night when
        it's out,
when the stars do slump through it. The force of nature is sexual
        too, but
when the stars do slump through it.

Finding out that your teenager is pregnant can be stressful.

7.

Just then
something like a hot potato
falls
from the cataclysmic sphere,
ripping elements of the perceptible
in half
and bearing the teeth
that might have already been there but had been hidden
behind the big picture
of a smile of mine
and perceived only barely in those extremely fleeting moments
in which I became a witness to the dubious impossibility
of being a happy kitten.

8.

What's wrong with me?

What could I have done to deserve
this?

How could this happen?

Why am I passing?

What is my problem?

Is the point of life to "get stuff done"?

Is the point of life to survive it?

Do I like my job?

Can you please help my husband or wife
understand what is happening to me?

Am I changing into another person?

Who are my friends?

     I'll give an example:

Why can't I just eat my waffle?

Why can't I come in peace?

How come every time I urinate, I shudder?

What do I mean by "self-destruction"?

     I'll be more precise:

When will this pain end?

What can I do about nausea and vomiting?

How can I quit my job without giving two weeks notice?

Why am I behaving like this?

What do I want out of the various things
I put time into?

Why do I bother?

What will help to curb excessive dreaming?

What's my Lyme disease risk?

Why do I feel so squeezed?

9.

Workers of the world, come on already.

Hell is here, and now
the biggest question in the universe is no longer
         what now?
         but
         what happened to the likelihood of there being
a what-now?
The police came in long ago,
         knocking people around
         away from the door

and battering women
where they stood.   What more do you need
to know to know
what you don't know already. What even do you
do? I do a bunch of leg and back stretches and float away
on a gentle breeze. The breeze is sickly sweet.
It blows your ceaseless labor your way,
                    and your life goes your way too.

To build the house of death,
that is my mission for the day. But who will dream in this
      house
if I build it?   Policemen and the friends of policemen
are known to have no dreams. Their nights are full of
      nightmares
and their days are full of sensuous detail, and that is hell for
      them
too.

                    Go now, bossmen,
                      into the starry sky!
                    Come now down
                      with a splat!

            Hell requires of you mighty powers
            unlike the powers of the court,
                  but not so unlike the powers of the court
            that they could not be used in the court, and so
            the powers that hell requires can be understood
            as universally binding, but not here. They become
                  applicable
                      elsewhere.

From star to star, woman to woman,
our class up and hops to another, while I, weepy,
cram self-discovery down my own throat, gripping
the joystick and waggling it frantically, unconcerned with the
    actual action
on the screen but fully absorbed in the back and forth of my
    hand
in relation to the action.

          Swelled to the size of a melon.

How can you align yourself with someone
in hell? Do you know what they do and don't do there? They
    ascend
the rocky slopes as if they were mountain goats, as if
they thought they would suffer more slightly as anything other
    than anything
other than human.

Lifted off or landed.

Lighter to ever lighter.

Up the mimic firmament, and under the double numbers.

The inapprehensible, and by extension, non-human universe
expands ever inward, toward a big bag with a jewel in it. That's
    your hand in the bag,
always pulling the jewel out.   Hell is getting your hand stuck in
    the bag
and being made to work with a bag on your hand, typing away

in a cold apartment for the limited time of a day, self-employed
    by a fraction
of a percentage. You kicked your boss in the shin. I kicked my
    boss in the bristling rift.
Who wins the free turkey dinner?

I do.

I can barely operate the brittle linguistic means of perpetuating
    power relations.
I can barely shift
the oxygen in and out of my lungs. In space,
my bosses are constructing a feeling
where it hurts the most. They have a heart
and it's mine, beating
in the dark suburbs of the moment before sleep
when I like to lie there and listen to the gentle lub-dub sounds
of my blood as it travels this way and that but never back, never
out of the groove into which it was first consciously poured.

Death is common in space.
My bosses all starve up there,
circling the sun forever in a ship that looks like a Hummer but
    bigger
and bright blue like the Earth's water,
impervious to radiation but not to the knowledge
that other people have of one, if one is understood
to be piggybacking on the distinction between here
and over there, merely alone, gazing at the stars
from a porthole and whispering childhood secrets to the world,
your new imaginary friend and confidante,
the only thing in your part of space

that's shaped like a mashed-up face, like the face of an employee
in the break room, sipping bitter coffee
with your finger in the coffee.

World,
you may be the best blue planet but you're far from my best
    friend,
for you only do whatever I do by virtue of my seeing you, and

you only see me as I do you. You are merely the nearest planet
    to the sun
as I am nearest the sun, as I am the smallest number that's both
a square and a cube –

what number am I?

II.

BLOODLESS GRAMMATICAL UNITS

NAPS

Steven "Baby Cakes" Zultanski
  dreams of cradling his ovum
  as he suckles at the nipple of
Steven "Little Man" Zultanski
  who dreams of cradling his sperm
  as he suckles at the nipple of
Steven "Cuddle Bunny" Zultanski
  who dreams of cradling his zygote
  as he suckles at the nipple of
Steven "Munchkin" Zultanski
  who dreams of cradling his blastocoel
  as he suckles at the nipple of
Steven "Huggy Bear" Zultanski
  who dreams of cradling his blastocyst
  as he suckles at the nipple of
Steven "Giggles" Zultanski
  who dreams of cradling his yolk sac
  as he suckles at the nipple of
Steven "String Bean" Zultanski
  who dreams of cradling his embryo
  as he suckles at the nipple of
Steven "Booger" Zultanski
  who dreams of cradling his limb buds
  as he suckles at the nipple of
Steven "Piglet" Zultanski
  who dreams of cradling his heartbeat
  as he suckles at the nipple of
Steven "Bubbaloo" Zultanski

who dreams of cradling his facial features

as he suckles at the nipple of

Steven "Little Bear" Zultanski

who dreams of cradling his amniotic sac

as he suckles at the nipple of

Steven "Sweetpea" Zultanski

who dreams of cradling his fetus

as he suckles at the nipple of

Steven "Boobie Monster" Zultanski

who dreams of cradling his tooth buds

as he suckles at the nipple of

Steven "Pickle" Zultanski

who dreams of cradling his red blood cells

as he suckles at the nipple of

Steven "Dumpling" Zultanski

who dreams of cradling his lanugo

as he suckles at the nipple of

Steven "Love Bug" Zultanski

who dreams of cradling his meconium

as he suckles at the nipple of

Steven "Smoochie" Zultanski

who dreams of cradling his fetal skin

as he suckles at the nipple of

Steven "Peanut" Zultanski

who dreams of cradling his EEG movement

as he suckles at the nipple of

Steven "My Little Caboose" Zultanski

who dreams of cradling his eyelashes

as he suckles at the nipple of

Steven "BooBoo" Zultanski

who dreams of cradling his aveoli

as he suckles at the nipple of

Steven "Snuggles" Zultanski

    who dreams of cradling his thalamic brain connections

    as he suckles at the nipple of

Steven "Puddin Pop" Zultanski

    who dreams of cradling his bones

    as he suckles at the nipple of

Steven "Monkey Baby" Zultanski

    who dreams of cradling his nipple buds

    as he suckles at the nipple of

Steven "Squish" Zultanski

    who dreams of cradling his head hair

    as he suckles at the nipple of

Steven "Noodle" Zultanski

    who dreams of cradling his newborn

    as he suckles at the nipple of

Steven "Stinky Butt" Zultanski

    who dreams of cradling his umbilical cord

    as he suckles at the nipple of

Steven "Big Man" Zultanski

    who dreams of cradling his placenta

    as he suckles at the nipple of

Steven "Baby Doll" Zultanski.

NUTS

That nut
Steven "George Washington" Zultanski
        fell from the Chain Cent tree
        into the field of that nut
Steven "John Adams" Zultanski
        who fell from the Wreath Cent tree
        into the field of that nut
Steven "Thomas Jefferson" Zultanski
        who fell from the Liberty Cap Cent tree
        into the field of that nut
Steven "James Madison" Zultanski
        who fell from the Draped Bust Cent tree
        into the field of that nut
Steven "James Monroe" Zultanski
        who fell from the Classic Head Cent tree
        into the field of that nut
Steven "John Quincy Adams" Zultanski
        who fell from the Coronet Cent tree
        into the field of that nut
Steven "Andrew Jackson" Zultanski
        who fell from the Braided Hair Cent tree
        into the field of that nut
Steven "Martin van Buren" Zultanski
        who fell from the Flying Eagle Cent tree
        into the field of that nut
Steven "William H. Harrison" Zultanski
        who fell from the Indian Head Cent tree
        into the field of that nut

Steven "John Tyler" Zultanski
     who fell from the Lincoln Wheat Cent tree
     into the field of that nut
Steven "James K. Polk" Zultanski
     who fell from the 1943 Steel Cent tree
     into the field of that nut
Steven "Zachary Taylor" Zultanski
     who fell from the Lincoln Memorial Cent tree
     into the field of that nut
Steven "Millard Fillmore" Zultanski
     who fell from the Shield Nickel tree
     into the field of that nut
Steven "Franklin Pierce" Zultanski
     who fell from the Liberty Head Nickel tree
     into the field of that nut
Steven "James Buchanan" Zultanski
     who fell from the Buffalo Nickel tree
     into the field of that nut
Steven "Abraham Lincoln" Zultanski
     who fell from the Jefferson Nickel tree
     into the field of that nut
Steven "Andrew Johnson" Zultanski
     who fell from the Draped Bust Dime tree
     into the field of that nut
Steven "Ulysses S. Grant" Zultanski
     who fell from the Capped Bust Dime tree
     into the field of that nut
Steven "Rutherford B. Hayes" Zultanski
     who fell from the Seated Liberty Dime tree
     into the field of that nut
Steven "James Garfield" Zultanski
     who fell from the Barber Dime tree

into the field of that nut
Steven "Chester A. Arthur" Zultanski
who fell from the Mercury Dime tree
into the field of that nut
Steven "Grover Cleveland" Zultanski
who fell from the Roosevelt Dime tree
into the field of that nut
Steven "Benjamin Harrison" Zultanski
who fell from the Draped Bust Quarter tree
into the field of that nut
Steven "Grover Cleveland (2nd term)" Zultanski
who fell from the Capped Bust Quarter tree
into the field of that nut
Steven "William McKinley" Zultanski
who fell from the Seated Liberty Quarter tree
into the field of that nut
Steven "Theodore Roosevelt" Zultanski
who fell from the Standing Liberty Quarter tree
into the field of that nut
Steven "William H. Taft" Zultanski
who fell from the Washington Quarter tree
into the field of that nut
Steven "Woodrow Wilson" Zultanski
who fell from the Flowing Hair Half Dollar tree
into the field of that nut
Steven "Warren G. Harding" Zultanski
who fell from the Draped Bust Half Dollar tree
into the field of that nut
Steven "Calvin Coolidge" Zultanski
who fell from the Capped Bust Half Dollar tree
into the field of that nut
Steven "Herbert Hoover" Zultanski

who fell from the Seated Liberty Half Dollar tree
into the field of that nut
Steven "Franklin D. Roosevelt" Zultanski
who fell from the Barber Half Dollar tree
into the field of that nut
Steven "Harry S. Truman" Zultanski
who fell from the Walking Liberty Half Dollar tree
into the field of that nut
Steven "Dwight D. Eisenhower" Zultanski
who fell from the Franklin Half Dollar tree
into the field of that nut
Steven "John F. Kennedy" Zultanski
who fell from the Kennedy Half Dollar tree
into the field of that nut
Steven "Lyndon B. Johnson" Zultanski
who fell from the Silver Dollar tree
into the field of that nut
Steven "Richard Nixon" Zultanski
who fell from the Seated Liberty Dollar tree
into the field of that nut
Steven "Gerald Ford" Zultanski
who fell from the Gold Dollar tree
into the field of that nut
Steven "Jimmy Carter" Zultanski
who fell from the Morgan Dollar tree
into the field of that nut
Steven "Ronald Reagan" Zultanski
who fell from the Peace Dollar tree
into the field of that nut
Steven "George H. W. Bush" Zultanski
who fell from the Eisenhower Dollar tree
into the field of that nut

Steven "Bill Clinton" Zultanski
    who fell from the Anthony Dollar tree
    into the field of that nut
Steven "George W. Bush" Zultanski
    who fell from the Sacagawea Dollar tree
    into the field of that nut
Steven "Barack Obama" Zultanski
    who is still in mid-air.

NODS

Steven "Skull Like an Afghani Terrorist" Zultanski
        gives terrorist head
        as hit-or-miss as a cluster bomb to
Steven "Skull Like a Vietnamese Communist" Zultanski
        who gives communist head
        as hot as napalm to
Steven "Skull Like an Italian Fascist" Zultanski
        who gives fascist head
        as automatic as a machine-gun to
Steven "Skull Like a Panamanian Drug Trafficker" Zultanski
        who gives drug trafficker head
        as likely to burn through steel as an incendiary bomb to
Steven "Skull Like a Japanese Imperialist" Zultanski
        who gives imperialist head
        as radioactive as Little Boy to
Steven "Skull Like a German Nazi" Zultanski
        who gives Nazi head
        as high capacity as a cookie to
Steven "Skull Like a Iraqi Insurgent" Zultanski
        who gives insurgent head
        as bunker-busting as a bunker-buster to
Steven "Skull Like a British Royalist" Zultanski
        who gives royalist head
        as round as a cannonball to
Steven "Skull Like a Palestinian Freedom Fighter" Zultanski
        who gives freedom fighter head
        as smoky as white phosphorous to
Steven "Skull Like a Somalian Islamist" Zultanski

who gives Islamist head
as rapid-fire as a gatling gun to
Steven "Skull Like a Filipino Anti-Imperialist" Zultanski
who gives anti-imperialist head
as inaccurately as a musket to
Steven "Skull Like an American Black Radical" Zultanski
who gives black radical head
as explosive as C-4 to
Steven "Skull Like a Libyan Revolutionary" Zultanski
who gives revolutionary head
as tactical as an AGM-88 HARM to
Steven "Skull Like a Mexican Citizen" Zultanski
who gives citizen head
as pointy as a bayonet to
Steven "Skull Like a Bosnian Nationalist" Zultanski
who gives nationalist head
as precise as precision-guided munitions to
Steven "Skull Like a Pakistani Jihadist" Zultanski
who gives jihadist head
as unmanned as a Predator drone to
Steven "Skull Like a Russian Communist" Zultanski
who threatens mutual assured destruction
as apocalyptic as American capitalist head.

NETS

Steven "British Pound" Zultanski
    nets a Norwegian
    and transfers it to
Steve "Norwegian Krone" Zultanski
    who nets a Swede
    and transfers it to
Steven "Swedish Krona" Zultanski
    who nets a Pole
    and transfers it to
Steven "Polish Złoty" Zultanski
    who nets a Belarusian
    and transfers it to
Steven "Belarusian Ruble" Zultanski
    who nets a Russian
    and transfers it to
Steven "Russian Ruble" Zultanski
    who nets a Chinese person
    and transfers it to
Steve "Chinese Renminbi Yuan" Zultanski
    who nets a Philippino
    and transfers it to
Steve "Philippine Peso" Zultanski
    who nets a Papua New Guinean
    and transfers it to
Steven "Papua New Guinean Pina" Zultanski
    who nets an Australian
    and transfers it to
Steven "Australian Dollar" Zultanski

who nets an Indonesian

and transfers it to

Steven "Indonesian Rupiah" Zultanski

who nets an Indian

and transfers it to

Steven "Indian Rupee" Zultanski

who nets a Pakistani

and transfers it to

Steven "Pakistani Rupee" Zultanski

who nets an Iranian

and transfers it to

Steven "Iranian Rial" Zultanski

who nets a Saudi

and transfers it to

Steven "Saudi Riyal" Zultanski

who nets a Sudanese person

and transfers it to

Steven "Sudanese Pound" Zultanski

who nets a Chadian

and transfers it to

Steven "Central African CFA Franc" Zultanski

who nets a Libyan

and transfers it to

Steven "Libyan Dinar" Zultanski

who nets an Algerian

and transfers it to

Steven "Algerian Dinar" Zultanski

who nets a Malian

and transfers it to

Steven "West African CFA Franc" Zultanski

who nets a Guinean

and transfers it to

Steven "Guinean Franc" Zultanski
  who nets a Brazilian
  and transfers it to
Steven "Brazilian Real" Zultanski
  who nets a Venezuelan
  and transfers it to
Steven "Venezuelan Bolivar" Zultanski
  who nets a Cuban
  and transfers it to
Steven "Cuban Peso" Zultanski
  who nets a Mexican
  and transfers it to
Steven "Mexican Peso" Zultanski
  who nets an American
  and transfers it to
Steven "United States Dollar" Zultanski
  who nets an Irish person
  and transfers it to
Steven "Euro" Zultanski.

NAILS

Private Steven Zultanski
        digs his nails
        into the palms of
Seaman Recruit Steven Zultanski
        who digs his nails
        into the wrists of
Airman Basic Steven Zultanski
        who digs his nails
        into the arms of
Private E-2 Steven Zultanski
        who digs his nails
        into the elbows of
Seaman Apprentice Steven Zultanski
        who digs his nails
        into the shoulders of
Private First Class Steven Zultanski
        who digs his nails
        into the throat of
Airman Steven Zultanski
        who digs his nails
        into the Adam's apple of
Seaman Steven Zultanski
        who digs his nails
        into the chin of
Lance Corporal Steven Zultanski
        who digs his nails
        into the cheeks of
Airman First Class Steven Zultanski

who digs his nails
into the lips of
Specialist Steven Zultanski
who digs his nails
into the gums of
Corporal Steven Zultanski
who digs his nails
into the tongue of
Petty Officer Third Class Steven Zultanski
who digs his nails
into the nose of
Senior Airman Steven Zultanski
who digs his nails
into the eyes of
Sergeant Steven Zultanski
who digs his nails
into the brow of
Drill Sergeant Steven Zultanski
who digs his nails
into the scalp of
Petty Officer Second Class Steven Zultanski
who digs his nails
into the temples of
Staff Sergeant Steven Zultanski
who digs his nails
into the ears of
Petty Officer First Class Steven Zultanski
who digs his nails
into the neck of
Technical Sergeant Steven Zultanski
who digs his nails
the upper-back of

Sergeant First Class Steven Zultanski
    who digs his nails
    into the armpits of
Chief Petty Officer Steven Zultanski
    who digs his nails
    into the middle-back of
Gunnery Sergeant Steven Zultanski
    who digs his nails
    into the lower-back of
Master Sergeant Steven Zultanski
    who digs his nails
    into the buttocks of
First Sergeant Steven Zultanski
    who digs his nails
    into the anus of
Senior Chief Petty Officer Steven Zultanski
    who digs his nails
    into the legs of
Senior Master Sergeant Steven Zultanski
    who digs his nails
    into the calves of
Sergeant Major Steven Zultanski
    who digs his nails
    into the ankles of
Command Sergeant Major Steven Zultanski
    who digs his nails
    into the soles of
Master Chief Petty Officer Steven Zultanski
    who digs his nails
    into the toes of
Master Gunnery Sergeant Steven Zultanski
    who digs his nails

into the feet of
Chief Master Sergeant Steven Zultanski
who digs his nails
into shins of
Command Chief Master Sergeant Steven Zultanski
who digs his nails
into the knees of
Sergeant Major of the Army Steven Zultanski
who digs his nails
into the thighs of
Master Chief Petty Officer of the Navy Steven Zultanski
who digs his nails
into the scrotum of
Master Chief Petty Officer of the Coast Guard Steven Zultanski
who digs his nails
into the penis of
Sergeant Major of the Marine Corps. Steven Zultanski
who digs his nail
into the waist of
Chief Master Sergeant of the Air Force Steven Zultanski
who digs his nails
into the belly of
Chief Warrant Officer 1 Steven Zultanski
who digs his nails
into the belly-button of
Chief Warrant Officer 2 Steven Zultanski
who digs his nails
into the chest of
Chief Warrant Officer 3 Steven Zultanski
who digs his nails
into the nipples of
Chief Warrant Officer 4 Steven Zultanski

who digs his nails

into the heart of

Chief Warrant Officer 5 Steven Zultanski

who digs his nails

into the lungs of

Second Lieutenant Steven Zultanski

who digs his nails

into the stomach of

Ensign Steven Zultanski

who digs his nails

into the pancreas of

First Lieutenant Steven Zultanski

who digs his nails

into the pancreatic duct of

Lieutenant Junior Grade Steven Zultanski

who digs his nails

into the common bile duct of

Captain Steven Zultanski

who digs his nails

into the gall bladder of

Commodore Commander Steven Zultanski

who digs his nails

into the large intestine of

Flag Officer Colonel Steven Zultanski

who digs his nails

into the small intestine of

Lieutenant Steven Zultanski

who digs his nails

into the liver of

Major Steven Zultanski

who digs his nails

into the diaphragm of

Lieutenant Commander General Steven Zultanski
    who digs his nails
    into the spleen of
Lieutenant Colonel Steven Zultanski
    who digs his nails into
    the left kidney of
Commander Steven Zultanski
    who digs his nails
    into the descending colon of
Colonel Steven Zultanski
    who digs his nails
    into the right kidney of
Brigadier General Steven Zultanski
    who digs his nails
    into the ascending colon of
Rear Admiral Lower Half Steven Zultanski
    who digs his nails
    into the cecum of
Major General Steven Zultanski
    who digs his nails
    into the appendix of
Rear Admiral Upper Half Steven Zultanski
    who digs his nails
    into the ureter of
Lieutenant General Steven Zultanski
    who digs his nails
    into the bladder of
Vice Admiral Steven Zultanski
    who digs his nails
    into the urethra of
General Steven Zultanski
    who digs his nails

into the testicles of
Admiral Steven Zultanski
who digs his nails
into the rectum of
Army Chief of Staff Steven Zultanski
who digs his nails
into the inferior vena cava of
Chief of Naval Operations Steven Zultanski
who digs his nails
into the superior vena cava of
Commandant of the Coast Guard Steven Zultanski
who digs his nails
into the aortic valve of
Commandant of the Marine Corps. Steven Zultanski
who digs his nails
into the aorta of
Air Force Chief of Staff Steven Zultanski
who digs his nails
into the abdominal aorta of
General of the Army Steven Zultanski
who digs his nails
into the inferior mesenteric artery of
Fleet Admiral Steven Zultanski
who digs his nails
into the pelvis of
General of the Air Force Steven Zultanski
who digs his nails
into the spine of
Combatant Commander Steven Zultanski
who digs his nails
into the skull of
Secretary of Defense Steven Zultanski

who digs his nails
into the brain of
Commander-in-Chief Steven Zultanski.

/

COLOPHON

Manufactured in an edition of 500 copies in the fall of 2010 by BookThug. Distributed in Canada by the Literary Press Group: www.lpg.ca. Distributed in the United States by Small Press Distribution: www.spdbooks.org. Shop online at . www.bookthug.ca

BOOK
PRODUCTION
WAR ECONOMY
STANDARD

Type + design by Jay MillAr